SALEM

MW00958083

TRIALS

A History from Beginning to End

Copyright © 2021 by Hourly History.

All rights reserved.

Table of Contents

Introduction

The Salem Witch Trials took place in the town of Salem in 1692-1693. Salem, which was located in the British colony of Massachusetts in North America, was founded and governed by Puritans, an austere Christian sect that had sought refuge in North America only about 70 years prior. The ordeal began when a small group of young women, most of them between twelve and twenty years of age, began accusing members of their community of using witchcraft to harm or torment them.

For the Puritans, life was a constant battle between the forces of good and evil; they believed that the Devil stalked them, constantly trying to tempt them away from their God. Those who gave in to his temptations had the ability to secure special powers, making them witches. What was more, once one person became a witch and entered into allegiance with the Devil, the Puritans believed that they would assist the Devil in securing more souls. Therefore, the threat posed by witches within the Salem community felt very real and incredibly dangerous for the people at the time.

At the time of the Witch Trials, many aspects of life in Massachusetts and in Salem specifically were changing. In large part, as the first generation of Puritan migrants passed away, elders feared that the younger generations who had never known persecution in Britain were beginning to stray from the strict rules and rituals of Puritanism. What was more, issues of gender, race, politics, and religion all came together to create the conditions necessary for such a tragic event to take place.

By the time the Salem Witch Trials ended, more than two hundred people had been accused. The accusations likely haunted them for the rest of their lives. Furthermore, nineteen people were hanged, one person was crushed to death, and five more died in prison.

In the aftermath of this tragic event, Salem tried for generations to move on and forget, but the memory of these disturbing events stayed with them. Eventually, Salem came to terms with what happened through memorialization and education. It also remains one of the most infamous events in American history, recreated in many works of literature and film.

Chapter One

The Puritans of the Mayflower

"God is the highest good of the reasonable creature. The enjoyment of him is our proper; and is the only happiness with which our souls can be satisfied. To go to heaven, fully to enjoy God, is infinitely better than the most pleasant accommodations here."

—Jonathan Edwards, Puritan minister

In order to understand the Salem Witch Trials, we must first understand the society in which they occurred. The trials took place in the British colony of Massachusetts in a community of Puritan people. The Puritans were a Christian sect that appeared in the mid-sixteenth century.

The emergence of the Puritans was part of the longer history of the Protestant Reformation and religion in the early modern era. The Protestant Reformation began in 1517 when a German

Augustinian monk named Martin Luther posted his *Ninety-five Theses*, which was essentially a list of accusations against the Catholic Church. He alleged that the Catholic Church had strayed too far from the teachings of Jesus Christ and the Bible and needed to be reformed. His actions ignited a powder-keg in Europe, causing massive societal, political, and of course religious upheaval.

The myriad causes and consequences of the Protestant Reformation are too complex for the scope of this narrative. That said, one of the major reasons that the Reformation spread so vastly was the invention of the printing press and the dissemination of all kinds of knowledge, not the least of which the Bible itself. As more and more people read the Bible, they realized that many Catholic practices and doctrines were not strictly biblically based. Leaders at the time also recognized the advantages to be gained by breaking away from the control of the Catholic Church and the Papacy.

After the beginning of the Reformation, new Christian churches and church organizations struggled into being. The Puritans were a result of that phenomenon as well as the English Reformation. Legend holds that King Henry VIII of England broke from Catholicism to form his own Church of England because Pope Clement VII denied his request for an annulment in 1527. However, the social, political, and religious context of this event are far more complicated than that, though again, we do not have the space to explore the details in this narrative.

This religious schism caused massive upheaval in Britain (and the rest of Europe), as subsequent British monarchs wavered between Catholicism and Protestantism. Meanwhile, as this turmoil ensued, different groups of British citizens disagreed with how the religious reforms proceeded. Many agreed that the Roman Catholic Church had strayed too far from actual biblical doctrine, but they disagreed with the steps that the Church of England had taken to rectify the problem. They believed that more action was needed.

It was largely because of this belief that Calvinism, the origin of Puritanism, was founded by John Calvin early in the Reformation. Calvinists believed that more extreme reforms of the Catholic Church were necessary in order to live up to the standards that they believed God set forth for his people in the Bible. Puritans were similar to Calvinists in their beliefs; chiefly, what differentiated them from Calvinists was that they came later and arose out of dissatisfaction with the Church of England rather than Catholicism directly. They believed that the Reformation within Britain had not gone far enough either and that too many vestiges of Catholic, non-biblical teachings and practices remained.

As complex events unfolded in Britain, Puritans found themselves constantly caught in the fray. Whether the monarch on the throne was leading the Church of England or temporarily brought the country back under Catholic jurisdiction, the Puritans were outliers and experienced persecution.

During the reign of King James I during the first two decades of the seventeenth century, many Puritans migrated to the Netherlands, where they could practice their religious beliefs more freely. However, life was not perfect in the Netherlands. As time went on, the Puritans watched their children become more and more Dutch in culture. They feared that the influence the Netherlands had on their children would usurp their own. What was more, most of them had been farmers in Britain. When they moved to the Netherlands, they settled in cities and had to become laborers of one sort or another. As a whole, they longed for their old life.

Therefore, the decision was made to attempt a settlement in North America. This venture was anything but easy. In 1620, 102 passengers set sail on the *Mayflower*. After ten grueling weeks, they landed in present-day Massachusetts and founded Plymouth Colony. They landed in November, which was most unfortunate since the winters in New England were (and are) brutal. Only half of the original *Mayflower* passengers survived until the spring, and they did so only because of the generous help of local native peoples.

After surviving the initial winter, the Puritans were eventually successful in establishing a settlement in the New World. Within a couple of years, the population was increasing. In 1629, King Charles granted a charter for the Massachusetts Bay Colony. The following year, the Great Puritan Migration began, which lasted about ten years. Even after 1640, the Puritan population continued to expand in Massachusetts, but it was due more to births than migration.

Life in New England was not easy, and the fact that the Puritans managed not only to survive but also to thrive is a testament to their work ethic. While land was ample and fertile, winters were extremely harsh. Most Puritans spent almost all of their time during the warmer months working toward growing food and producing basic necessities like clothing. The rest of their time was spent in worship.

The Puritan worldview dictated everything about their lives. Puritans believed that they had a responsibility to create God's ideal community on earth and that they had been specially appointed by God to do it. If they were successful in this endeavor, God would act favorably toward them, but if they failed, it would be due to their own shortcomings and God's wrath over their failings.

Puritans' eschatological views were complex, and they changed over time. Generally speaking, Puritans believed in the Second Coming. This meant that they believed that history was preordained and that sometime in the future (typically, they thought the near future), Jesus Christ would return to earth, purify the world from sin and sinners, and establish his kingdom on earth for all eternity. Ostensibly, this was a hopeful outlook: war, pain, struggle, and suffering would soon disappear in favor of a literal heaven on earth. But the Puritans also held that it would only happen once the process was begun by his followers themselves. Therefore, it became their responsibility to purify the earth in preparation for his coming.

In addition, Puritans believed in the predestination of souls. This meant that they believed that God had already determined who was to be saved and ascend to heaven and who was damned to be cast into hell to suffer for all eternity. While on the surface this may seem freeing (the idea that there is nothing you can do to "earn" God's grace), in reality, it functioned as a powerful mechanism of social control. Puritans were compelled to conform in order to demonstrate to their society that they were among the blessed and not the damned and to prevent ostracization and even ex-communication. It became an even more powerful force in the New World since there was nowhere else to go should your community decide you are dangerous.

In terms of day-to-day life, this led to an austere and somber way of living. Puritans did not celebrate secular holidays or birthdays, nor did they even celebrate most religious holidays like Christmas or saints' feast days. This was in stark contrast to most of the Christian world during this time; local feast days led to outlandish revelry that often lasted for days. Likewise, they did not believe in indulging children; rather, it was parents' responsibility to steel their children to the evil in the world by disciplining their natural inclinations for outward expressions of joy. Dancing and other such activities were typically forbidden. What was more, around the time of the Salem Witch Trials, Puritan society was becoming stricter, partially in response to what they saw as growing encroachments on their independence.

In stark contrast to Catholicism at the time, Puritans strongly encouraged reading the Bible, which meant that the Puritans had a strikingly high rate of literacy for the time, even among women, and established some of North America's first schools. One way that the Puritans influenced what would become American culture was in their belief in independence of mind and thought and the importance of interpreting the Bible (which led to interpreting other things) for oneself. The role of Puritanism in the establishment of the United States is a fascinating and complicated topic, another one that is too big for the scope of this narrative.

Many people wrongly believe that since the Puritans journeyed to the New World in order to seek freedom to practice their religion, they therefore promoted religious freedom, but this was simply not the case. Puritans did not outright ban other faiths, but they did often persecute or ostracize people of other Christian sects.

In addition, Puritans were very concerned about outside influences on their society, particularly on its young members. One of the reasons why they migrated in the first place was to escape those kinds of influences, so they became extremely protective of their insular communities in the New World. This is one of the reasons why the trials occurred when they did: as the non-Puritan population in the region grew, Puritans became fearful and developed an almost pathological desire to root out dissent and opposition.

In the next chapter, we will zoom in on the late seventeenth century and the particular circumstances and events that created the Salem Witch Trials.

Chapter Two

Life in Colonial New England

"But now having seen him which is invisible I fear not what man can do unto me."

—Anne Hutchinson

Just as it is important to understand the Puritan society in which the Salem Witch Trials took place, it is also necessary to look at the world in which that society existed. British North America saw remarkable development throughout the seventeenth century, and in part, it was this rapid growth that helped cause the Salem Witch Trials.

The first permanent British colony—Virginia—was established in 1607. Thirteen years later, the first Puritans landed at Massachusetts Bay. Within twenty years, Maryland, Rhode Island, Connecticut, New Hampshire, and Delaware had all been established, not to mention growth within Massachusetts Bay itself. In addition, New Amsterdam was also settled by the Dutch nearby; it would become New York, another British colony, in the 1660s.

With all of these new settlements came many people, most of them migrants from Britain and enslaved persons from Africa. Obviously, the vast majority of these people were not Puritans. As time went on, the Puritans became concerned about encroachments on their lifestyle. Remember, they believed that they had been chosen by God to usher in his kingdom on earth by purifying society. Therefore, any threat to their ways of life was a matter of cosmic consequences.

In some other ways, however, Puritan life was compatible with developments happening around them, especially in economics. The Puritans originally came to North America chiefly to practice their religion freely and to re-establish the lifestyles they had in Britain before migrating to the Netherlands. Part of their doctrine also preached individualism, thrift, hard work, and independence. Many (if not most) of the non-Puritan people in North America were motivated to migrate by economic opportunity that was compatible with their religious lifestyle. Land was readily available in the New World, making it easy to acquire a farm. As the population grew, the colonies also began producing much of what they needed at home, including textiles and clothing, tools, even books and other luxury items. Tradesmen and their families migrated to establish businesses.

Therefore, the issue for the Puritans was not so much that all of these new arrivals were seeking economic independence, as the market slowly shifted toward capitalism and all it entails. It was that economics was the *primary* focus of these arrivals and their descendants. Meanwhile, the Puritans believed that they were on a mission to create a perfect, Godly society based on the teachings in the Bible. It was absolutely the most important aspect of their lives. As more and more people who did not adhere to their beliefs arrived in New England, that became more difficult. Failing at this meant failing God himself, a terrifying idea for the Puritan people. As the seventeenth century marched on, they felt more and more under threat from the outside world.

There were internal problems for the Puritans as well that made the late seventeenth century a turbulent time. Disagreements emerged about the role of the church in government, as well as land arrangements with the native peoples. Throughout the 1630s, an influential minister named Roger Williams continually clashed with Puritan leadership throughout Massachusetts Bay on these and other issues. His views about separation of church and state and freedom of religion were viewed as especially threatening to the Puritans' calling, and he was exiled in 1636. He did not leave, however, and instead founded Providence Plantation (which eventually became the Colony of Rhode Island) nearby.

An antinomian controversy also erupted in the 1630s involving conflicting views of Christian doctrine. It was a complicated conflict, but essentially, a woman named Anne Hutchinson spoke out against the teachings of some Puritan ministers. She believed that human actions did not matter in the face of the will of God. All Puritans believed firmly that they could not influence their own salvation (because it was predetermined by God), but Anne took that further.

By the end of the decade, the controversy had calmed, but not before the Puritans throughout Massachusetts Bay held a synod in which they agreed that more uniformity and consistency was needed between churches and ministers' messages. In some ways, this already revealed a diversion from the Puritans' original intent in migration. Prior to this, they believed and allowed churches to function relatively independently, serving the needs of their particular congregation. They also encouraged their members to read and interpret the Bible for themselves. This change in tone by the end of the 1630s tells us that they feared losing control over their populace and were becoming more insular.

While Puritan communities continued to see growth throughout the seventeenth century, they were becoming more and more surrounded by British people of other faiths, including Anabaptists, Baptists, Lutherans, Presbyterians, Quakers, and of course members of the Church of England.

Another major turning point for the Puritans came in the form of the Half-Way Covenant, which was issued in 1662. It tried to address problems involving church membership, specifically whether certain children could be baptized and become members of the Puritan church. While the changes that the Covenant brought were relatively minor, their importance lies more in what they signaled. Namely, that Puritanism was in decline and that the ideal held by many first-generation Puritans—that they would create an exclusive society of true Christian adherents—had failed. Although there were stricter congregations and periodic revivals of the apocalyptic mission, Puritanism was in decline.

More political changes came in 1691, mere months before the first accusations were made. The British government issued a new charter for the Colony of Massachusetts Bay in 1691, which went into effect in 1692. Increase Mather and his son Cotton Mather, both prominent Puritan ministers, played crucial roles in the drafting and institution of this charter and the new government for Massachusetts. Both believed firmly in the threat posed by witchcraft, having published books on the topic. With the issuance of the new charter, they were able to appoint members of law enforcement, including justices of the peace. Some of these appointees would eventually preside over the Salem Witch Trials.

On the local level, things in Salem and the surrounding towns were anything but peaceful. By the end of the seventeenth century, Salem was actually known for its high degree of conflict. Neighbors and co-parishioners frequently quarreled over property and grazing rights. They bickered about small debts and other matters, most of them trivial, almost constantly. They frequently found themselves involved in lawsuits against neighbors. This ongoing conflict was dangerously destructive, as it fed an atmosphere of paranoia and casual attitudes about issuing accusations. It made people constantly suspicious of their neighbors and defensive about their own actions. Although the conflict in the Salem Witch Trials was much more severe, this type of atmosphere made Salem the perfect place for such an event to occur.

The Salem Witch Trials occurred during this period of weakening for the Puritan people, which continued through the early eighteenth century. Historians generally agree that the Puritan era was completely over by the end of the 1740s. That said, there were other causes of the Salem Witch Trial. The next chapter will more closely examine the other complicated aspects of life that contributed to the trials.

Chapter Three

The Causes of the Salem Witch Trials

"Salem is in part a story of what happens when a set of unanswerable questions meets a set of unquestioned answers."

—Stacy Schiff

There were many elements of life in the late seventeenth century that contributed to the outbreak of the Salem Witch Trials. In fact, the social, political, racial, and religious circumstances at the time created something of a perfect storm for such an event.

In the last chapter, we discussed the growing populations of non-Puritans in and around Massachusetts and Salem itself. That presented many challenges to the Puritan people, especially involving concerns about the younger generations. It is telling that the first three women arrested on charges of witchcraft were all outsiders or non-conformists to Puritan life in some way.

For example, Sarah Good's father committed suicide when she was young, and even after she married, she was very poor. Not originally from Salem, she migrated to the town and mostly survived on charity. She had earned a reputation for being unpleasant, caustic, and argumentative, and she rarely attended church services.

Sarah Osborne also attended church services only sporadically. She was related through marriage to the wealthy John Putnam, Ann Putnam's father (Ann was one of the girls at the helm of the accusation). After Sarah's husband, Putnam's brother-in-law died, she married her indentured servant and denied her sons (who were also related to Putnam) their inheritance. This not only angered the family, but it completely flouted social and gender norms. The third woman was Tituba, who is discussed below.

At the time of the Salem Witch Trials, Massachusetts was also in the middle of a brutal Native American war, called King William's War. This conflict was marked by particular savagery on both sides. For the colonists, they were under constant threat of a surprise attack in which their town might be burned, they could be murdered and scalped, or taken prisoner and tortured. Undoubtedly, the residents of Salem, especially the young women, worried almost constantly about the violence happening around them. Remember, the Puritans saw the hand of divine power in everything. If so much violence was occurring around them, then the Devil was surely close at hand.

Salem itself was also going through major change. The municipality had split off into two distinct settlements: Salem Town and Salem Village. The population of the village was mostly subsistence farmers. The town, on the other hand, had a powerful merchant class tied to oceangoing since Salem is located on Massachusetts Bay and the Atlantic Ocean. The village, which was further inland, desired autonomy from the town, but the town depended on the village farmers both for food and as customers of many of their businesses (blacksmiths, carpenters, etc.).

It was Salem Village that elected Samuel Parris as their minister, who was a stern and strict Puritan. He would be at the center of the Witch Trials, and he was unpopular with Salem Town, further dividing the two entities. All of that said, the village was not completely independent and shared some institutions of government with the town, including courts.

Finally, Salem was experiencing a major feud at the time between two of its oldest families, the Putnams and the Porters. Both were powerful and wealthy, but in different ways that reflected the growing cultural divide between the residents of Salem. The Putnams were farmers and followed Puritan doctrine and lifestyle fairly closely. The Porters, on the other hand, were part of that growing merchant class. Years before the Witch Trials broke out, the Porters were responsible for flooding Putnam land, and the rift only grew from there after a lawsuit and ongoing conflict in which almost all residents of Salem took sides. Both families were at the heart of the first accusations.

Issues of race also contributed to the Salem Witch Trials. Race was a complicated issue at the time, and it is important to understand that our modern understanding of race was not the same during the seventeenth century. The ideas about race that were more concrete by the eighteenth and nineteenth centuries were still in flux and being formed in the seventeenth. This was especially true as peoples from all around the world became more mobile, especially around the

Atlantic Ocean. New England was directly tied to the rest of the world, and in many ways, the Puritans (especially those of the village) feared its influences. Race was largely understood in terms of "the other," meaning not necessarily people of other skin tones (although that was a major determining factor) but people whose lifestyles, languages, and religion were unfamiliar or even threatening.

All of these factors (as well as issues of gender) crystallized around the figure of Tituba, a Caribbean slave living amongst the Puritans who was central to the story of the Salem Witch Trials. As we will see, Tituba, who was still enslaved, was the very first person arrested for witchcraft. She had been an outcast in the community and had apparently engaged the young girls who made the first accusations in fortune-telling. Tituba fit the bill as an "other" in every way that one can imagine: she was enslaved, she was from a different culture, and she apparently still maintained practices that flew in the face of Puritan religious doctrine.

It is hard to miss the gender undertones in the Salem Witch Trials. While women were not the only people accused, they composed the majority (nearly 80%), they were the first to be accused, and the first accusations of witchcraft also originated with young women. What is more, witchcraft has traditionally been much more closely associated with women, both before and after Salem.

According to the Puritans' belief system, women were weaker than men not only physically but also morally; therefore, they were more susceptible to the temptations of the Devil in the first place. They also believed that the Devil tempted women more often than men because of their supposed moral inferiority. It is important to remember how real these ideas were for the Puritan people. Women especially saw their day-to-day lives fraught with constant temptations by the Devil, and they believed in the Devil's power to pull them away from God at any and every turn. Some of the women who confessed to witchcraft under interrogation may have actually believed that they had unwittingly given into the Devil and were guilty of witchcraft.

Of course, the wider gender context of the Salem Witch Trials and accusations of witchcraft generally are more complex. Throughout much of Western history, struggles between men and women for power and control have led to reactive, repressive tragedies like the Salem

Witch Trials. For complicated reasons, as the world around them changed, the Puritan leadership, composed of all men, was in part seeking to tighten their control over their society. Whether they realized it or not, the Witch Trials were at least partially a result of those kinds of changes.

In addition, the Salem Witch Trials were certainly not the first witch trials in Christian history or even Puritan history, nor were they the last. Although witch-hunts date back to ancient times and were not uncommon during the medieval period and Middle Ages, they peaked between about 1450-1750 in European societies, which means that Salem was actually at the tail end of the trend. They peaked in number and fervor, and then died down again for a period of time before spiking again.

Significantly, the English Witchcraft Act of 1542 codified the illegality of witchcraft. Then, the Pendle Witch Trials of 1612 condemned and executed ten alleged witches on murder charges. After that, in the middle of the English Civil War, a Puritan man named Matthew Hopkins led a massive witch-hunt movement in England that resulted in the executions of more than one hundred people between 1644 and 1646.

Hopkins' actions across the pond greatly influenced some of the first witch-hunts in North America, which incidentally did not take place in Salem. At least fifteen people were executed for practicing witchcraft before the 1660s. One of Hopkins' lasting legacies was the practice of asking accused witches for the names of accomplices, and while he did not invent this tactic, he popularized it at the time. In Britain and the colonies, this tactic would wreak much havoc and cause a cavalcade of accusations that destroyed many lives. This was certainly the case in Salem.

Finally, one additional contextual note. The Witch Trials began in the middle of an especially brutal winter. Winters in New England were always difficult, but the winter of 1691/92 was particularly cold, with seemingly endless snowfall, ice, and other conditions that made it difficult to live, let alone find comfort. While not a major element, it certainly contributed to the dismal outlook and atmosphere of the time. It is also possible that some Puritans saw the hard winter as proof of God's anger with them, although this idea is not proven.

It was in this context of upheaval, uncertainty, and change that the Salem Witch Trials occurred.

In the next chapter, we will detail how, when, and why the first accusations were made against Tituba, Sarah Good, and Sarah Osborne and what happened in the aftermath.

Chapter Four

The Accusations Begin

"I do not know that the devil goes about in my likeness to do any hurt."

—Sarah Osborne

The Salem Witch Trials began with the actions of children. The nine-year-old daughter of Reverend Samuel Parris, Betty, and her cousin Abigail Williams (eleven years old) began having "fits" in February of 1692. According to surviving accounts from witnesses of these fits, the girls screamed, convulsed, crawled, and writhed on the ground, and otherwise behaved strangely and disturbingly. They also had bruises, scratches, and other marks on their skin.

Soon, other young girls joined them, most notably Elizabeth Hubbard and Ann Putnam, Jr. (granddaughter of the patriarch of the Putnam family), both 12 years of age. According to some sources, the girls began behaving this way after they were caught allowing Tituba to teach them about fortune-telling.

Doctors and other people examined and observed the girls but could find no ailment or other cause for their behavior. As often happens, when science and reason fall short, the divine or mysterious is blamed, and that is exactly what happened. Many believed there could be no other explanation than the hand of the Devil through witchcraft. The girls were pressured to name their tormentors, and the first three accusations were cast.

One of the biggest mysteries that still surround the Salem Witch Trials is the behaviors of the accusers themselves. From what could they have been suffering or experiencing that would have caused such conduct? There are a couple of possibilities. Some experts in child psychology posit that it is possible that one or more of the first accusers was a victim of some kind of abuse. The behavior may have been a coping strategy for a child who was unable to verbalize the profundity of their trauma. If that is the case, it is likely some of the other children mimicked the original girls' behavior or were perhaps also suffering similar abuse.

Another possibility that was originally posited by scientists in the 1970s is that the girls suffered from convulsive ergotism. Basically, a fungus called ergot (from which LSD is derived) grows on rye, which the Puritans used to make bread. The particular circumstances needed for the fungus to grow were present at the time of the trials. Convulsive ergotism causes some of the symptoms the girls experienced, including fits and convulsions similar to seizures and crawling skin (the girls complained of being pinched and scratched). It can also cause hallucinations, which children in this Puritan society would almost certainly have attributed to witches.

Of course, there is also the possibility that the girls invented and playacted their symptoms for a variety of reasons. It is worth mentioning that Cotton Mather's book, *Memorable Providences: Relating to Witchcraft and Possessions*, was published just a few years before 1692. It contained a detailed description of the symptoms of young women possessed by witches, one that was eerily reminiscent of the behavior of Betty, Ann, and their other friends. Reading was a priority for the Puritans who valued education, and this book was widely circulated.

If it was the case that the first accusations occurred after the girls pretended to be bewitched, it is highly likely that what unfolded afterward was somewhat out of their hands. It is hard to imagine that a group of children would have had the forethought to know that their actions would have such dramatic and tragic consequences. It also seems entirely plausible that, after being caught in the act of wrongdoing (telling fortunes with Tituba) that they cried witchcraft to get out of trouble in such an austere and intolerant society. It would not be out of character with what we now know about child development and the stage of development that their brains were in at the time.

Regardless of the true cause, witchcraft was blamed, and the girls eventually identified three outsiders as witches. The identities of the accused shed some light on the context: as discussed previously, all three of them deviated in some way from Salem's societal norms and did not have strong family ties. They were natural suspects and easy targets. If the girls were pressured to reveal who in their community had bewitched them, these three women would have been the easiest targets. All three were quickly arrested.

Shortly after the accusations and arrests, the women faced grueling interrogations by the town magistrates—John Hathorne and Jonathan Corwin—without representation. These hearings began on March 1, 1592, and lasted several days. Tituba confessed to the crime of witchcraft (which could have had much to do with self-preservation, given her enslaved status and her race). She named the other two accused women as fellow witches, confirming the town's worst suspicions.

Many of the people who were accused of witchcraft wound up making confessions, either during their initial interrogations or later in the formal court. It can seem puzzling as to why, especially in our modern world where many people don't believe in witches anymore, at least not the kind that Salemites feared. It is best to understand this is the best option many of them had to save their lives. If a person denied being a witch and were convicted by the courts, they usually faced death. If a person confessed, and especially if they named others, they were more likely to be spared, especially if they showed genuine remorse and attempts to reconcile their sins. This was another factor that exacerbated the Salem Witch Trials.

Also in March, more accusations began to be made. This second round of accusations differed from the first; this time, the accused were not necessarily outcasts. One of the newly accused was Martha Corey who, unlike the first three women, was an active member of the Salem community and the church. However, she did not believe in witchcraft and was outspoken about her opinion that the girls were lying. She was accused by Ann Putnam, Jr. and another of Putnam's peers, Mercy Lewis, age 14. Mercy became a servant in Ann's house after moving to Salem from Maine, where her entire family had been killed in an attack by native peoples.

Dorothy Good, the young daughter of Sarah Good, was accused of witchcraft; the girls alleged that she practiced it alongside her mother. Dorothy was only four or five years old. At the time, witchcraft was believed to be largely a group activity; the Devil summoned his followers together. In part, this led to cascading accusations, as supposed witches were questioned not only about their own activities but also about those of others accused of witchcraft. Tragically, this child's testimony in front of magistrates ended up condemning her mother.

Finally, Rebecca Nurse was alleged to be a witch by Ann Putnam, Jr. Nurse was 71 years old at the time, and she would be one of the oldest people accused during the Salem Witch Trials. Her arrest also came as a shock, as she was a regular churchgoer and had a reputation for generosity and piety.

This second round of accusations was enormously troubling to the community, much more so than the first. Nurse and Corey were church members and well-respected. It was not so much that Salemites didn't believe the accusations; more so, they were terrified at the idea that the accusations were true. If the Devil was powerful enough to corrupt such upstanding members of the community and followers of God, then no one was safe. Certainly, this contributed to the sense of hysteria that soon permeated every aspect of Puritan life during the last weeks of the brutal winter.

Chapter Five

Mass Hysteria in Salem

"I can say before my eternal father I am innocent, and God will clear my innocency [sic]."

—Rebecca Nurse

As stated in the previous chapter, the events of early March shook the village and town of Salem. As the alleged witches were arrested, they were brought before local magistrates for questioning. They were not allowed representation by a lawyer and had to argue for themselves (even accused children). Several more accusations were made by more and more girls throughout the month of March, including two members of the Proctor family, John and Elizabeth, a married couple. In addition, cascading accusations began as those interrogated also started naming names.

As the hysteria grew, doubts also began to be cast. In early April, the Proctors' accuser, Mary

Warren, admitted to lying about the allegations of witchcraft. She was, however, a servant in the Proctor household and may have been coerced into retracting her accusations. She paid for her decision either way; she was herself accused of witchcraft shortly thereafter, on April 18, by some of the other young women and arrested. Nonetheless, her revelation that she and the other girls were acting out their fits caused some in the Salem community pause, though not enough to halt or even slow the arrests.

Several people were arrested after defending Rebecca Nurse. What this tells us is the level of conformity and fear that accompanied the accusations of witchcraft. Any dissent or refute of the charges of witchcraft very often led to arrest and accusations of one's own. No wonder it was so difficult to slow the proceedings, given the obvious risks involved in doing so, as the people of Salem saw what happened to Nurse's defenders. Mary Warren is another example of this kind of intense pressure at work.

At the end of April, perhaps the most shocking accusation to date was made. Several of the girls accused the former Salem minister, George Burroughs. He was arrested in Maine in late April and brought to Salem to stand trial.

During his time as minister, his wages were unpaid by the village, and he had to borrow money from Thomas Putnam to bury his wife in 1681. He left the village in 1683 without repaying his debts, but he had been gone almost a decade before the girls in Salem accused him and forced his return. He would be among those executed, and he famously recited the Lord's Prayer before he was hung. It was believed that a witch could not recite this prayer and thus represented another moment of doubt about the veracity of the accusations.

By the time of Burroughs' arrest, approximately twenty others had also been accused and arrested. But shortly thereafter, larger forces of government began to intervene in the events unfolding in Salem. Earlier that month, the new governor of Massachusetts Bay, Sir William Phipps, arrived in Boston with Increase Mather. Phipps convened a special court to deal with the accusations called a Court of Oyer and Terminer. Used at various times throughout British history, this was a special court appointed just to deal with a particular set of crimes (in this case, witchcraft). Commissioners were appointed and tasked with handling the matter swiftly and fairly.

Prior to this point, after being arrested, accused witches were questioned in front of the town's magistrates. Typically, they were then remanded to jail until they could stand trial. With the Court of Oyer and Terminer, the official phase of prosecutions began, as did deaths and executions.

Chapter Six

The First Executions

"The New Englanders are a People of God settled in those, which were once the Devil's Territories; and it may easily be supposed that the Devil was exceedingly disturbed, when he perceived such a People here accomplishing the Promise of old made unto our Blessed Jesus [sic]."

—Cotton Mather

By May, several additional young women joined the others in their accusations against neighbors and fellow members of the Salem community. The witch hunt also claimed its first victim: Sarah Osborne, one of the first people accused, died in prison on May 10, 1692.

Meanwhile, the Court of Oyer and Terminer appointed seven judges (all men). William Stoughton, a colonial administrator from outside Salem who would go on to serve as governor of Massachusetts Bay, was appointed as chief justice. Locally, Jonathan Corwin, Bartholomew Gedney, and John Hathorne, all Salem magistrates, were appointed. Finally, four others were also named to the Court: Nathaniel Saltonstall, Peter Sergeant, Samuel Sewall, and Wait Still Winthrop. Sewall had assisted with questioning already. Saltonstall would not serve long, leaving the court principally for his objection of the admission of "spectral evidence," which Stoughton and several of the others favored.

An ongoing question during the trials involved the inclusion of spectral evidence. Spectral evidence would become some of the most dramatic and memorable parts of the Trials. It is testimony from accusers or witnesses about the appearance of the accused's spirit to the witness apart from the accused's body. In other words, admitting this kind of testimony would allow the girls who made the accusations of witchcraft to testify that the spirits of the people they accused visited and tormented them, even if the alleged witch were in an entirely other location. As is obvious, this kind of evidence was dubious at best and practically impossible to refute. In the end, Stoughton supported its relevancy and generally allowed its admission as evidence. In addition, while Thomas Newton prosecuted the cases, no defense was provided or allowed for the accused persons.

The first person to stand trial before this court was Bridget Bishop, who was accused by five of the young women. Little is known of her, although she may have owned a tavern in the town of Salem. If she were in fact a tavern owner, it would have placed her in the category of unconventional women who flouted norms of Puritan society, many of whom were accused alongside Bishop. She was convicted on June 2 and hanged eight days later, the first person executed for witchcraft in the Salem Witch Trials.

After the execution of Bridget Bishop, the courts paused their proceedings, perhaps to grapple with the magnitude of their own actions. Officially, though, they sought advice from outsiders about how to proceed with the rest of the trials. Cotton Mather drafted a response, which is complicated, but when taken as a whole told the Court to proceed as they had been. On the surface, it appears to speak out against spectral evidence but, in the end, did nothing to stop it. It was at this time that Saltonstall resigned.

Hearings and trials resumed on June 30. Five women, including Rebecca Nurse and Sarah

Good, were hanged on July 19. Within the next month, grand juries indicted several people, and the Court held more trials. On August 19, five more alleged witches were hanged. Elizabeth Proctor would have been among them, but she was granted a stay of execution because she was pregnant. Her husband John, though, was not so lucky; he went to the gallows on the 19th.

Many would have thought that after more than ten deaths, the hysteria would have calmed, but that was not the case. In September, the grand jury indicted 18 more people on the charge of witchcraft, and the trials proceeded unabated. At the same time, the allegations of witchcraft were spreading to neighboring communities. In Ipswich, located several miles north of Salem, a woman named Rachel Clinton, a social outcast like Sarah Osborne, was also accused of witchcraft. Other communities were similarly affected.

It is difficult to imagine the magnitude of paranoia that must have permeated the town and village of Salem. Not only were the accusations of young girls being taken seriously, but many people were being executed. It was also hard to miss that the condemned were very often people who had feuded with the girls' families or had deviated from societal norms in some way. Undoubtedly, this sense of fear created an atmosphere of oppressive conformity, one that would outlast the trials themselves for decades to come.

Chapter Seven

Corey's Death by Pressing

"I saw the apparition of Giles Corey come and afflict me to write in his book and so he continued most dreadfully to hurt me by times beating me and almost breaking my back till the day of his examination . . . I verily believe in my heart that Giles Corey is a dreadful wizard."

—Testimony given in the Court of Oyer and Terminer

Two of the men hanged on August 19 were George Jacobs, Sr. and George Burroughs, the former minister of Salem. The very next day, Jacobs's granddaughter, Margaret Jacobs, recanted her testimony given earlier that month that led to their convictions and subsequent executions. She, too, had been accused of witchcraft and had named their names during questioning by the magistrates, most likely in an attempt to secure her own freedom.

Margaret Jacobs's situation is helpful in illustrating what this experience must have been like for some of those involved. While all of the details of her circumstances are not known, she was among both the accused and accusers. She had to choose between saving her own life and condemning that of her family member. While she was eventually acquitted, no doubt the trauma of the experience followed her for the rest of her life.

The situation only worsened for all of Salem as autumn approached. Grand juries handed down eighteen more indictments in early September. Then, on September 19, one of the most infamous and gruesome events of the trials occurred: the death of Giles Corey. Born in England in 1611, he came to Massachusetts early on during the Puritan Migration. The Salem Witch Trials was not his first experience with the law. About 15 years earlier, he beat one of his indentured servants so severely that the man eventually died. Using physical force against indentured servants was permitted at the time though, so he was eventually cleared of any charges.

When Corey appeared in court after being indicted, he refused to enter a plea of guilty or not guilty. This was a problem because under the laws in force at the time, without a plea he could not be tried. In an attempt to force him into a plea, the courts used a method called *peine forte et dure*. Corey was stripped of all clothing and forced to lay on his back with boards placed over his body. Then, heavy rocks and boulders were slowly placed on the boards. The idea was that the victim would relent and enter a plea under such incredible pain, but Corey did not give in. He refused to participate in anything about the trials and was slowly crushed to death.

Corey's indictment occurred around the same time that his wife, along with five others, was convicted of witchcraft. Witnessing her trial may have been a factor in his refusal to enter a plea; he may have seen himself as condemned one way or the other. After all, nine more people were convicted two days before he was crushed. His wife, along with seven others, were hanged on September 22, three days after Corey's death.

A turning point in the trials occurred in October. Perhaps because of the high number of convictions and executions, leaders began to speak out against the use of spectral evidence.

Spectral evidence accounted for many of the convictions and was some of the most sensational testimony given in the trials. It also kept the spotlight on the alleged victims, which may have been a factor in keeping them going for so long. One of the first to speak out against it was Increase Mather, Cotton Mather's father, who was himself a very famous Puritan minister and president of Harvard College at the time. He issued a statement on October 3, and five days later, Governor Phipps outlawed the use of spectral evidence by the Court of Oyer and Terminer.

The next phase of the Salem Witch Trials involved bureaucracy. By the end of October, Phipps intervened directly by dissolving the Court of Oyer and Terminer and releasing many of the people held in jail on witchcraft charges. He also forbade Salem officials from arresting any more people for allegedly practicing witchcraft. About a month later, a new Superior Court called the Superior Court of Judicature, overseen by the colonial administration for Massachusetts Bay, was established to try the remaining witches.

Chapter Eight

The Legacy of Witchcraft in Salem

"By 1892, enlightenment had progressed to the point where the Salem trials were simply an embarrassing blot on the history of New England. They were a part of the past that was best forgotten: a reminder of how far the human race had come in two centuries."

—Edmund Morgan

The dissolution of the Court of Oyer and Terminer did not end the hysteria in Salem, although it did slow things down significantly, especially after the local government was prohibited from making more arrests. The Trials could not have occurred in the first place if Salemites did not fervently believe in the existence of witches and the power of the Devil in their midst. Many genuinely believed, and undoubtedly most at least suspected, that the accusations were real. It is hard to know when the arrests would have slowed if the colonial government had not stepped in.

Further complicating matters was the tricky legal predicament that faced an accused person. If a person accused of witchcraft confessed, they had a much higher likelihood of keeping their life. Those who denied the accusations and were later convicted were the ones who were hanged. That meant that, in an effort to save their own lives, many people confessed who were not guilty. It presented a legal conundrum of what to do with the people who had confessed. Therefore, grappling with the end of the trials and returning to some semblance of normal life was difficult for everyone in Salem, particularly those who had been accused of and confessed to witchcraft.

On January 3, 1693, one of the most ardent supporters of the trials, Judge William Stoughton, attempted to follow through with the rest of the executions, including executing the several women who had been awarded stays of execution because of pregnancy. However, Phipps intervened directly, and the executions never took place. Stoughton resigned, and his departure from the proceedings marked another step toward the end of the trials and the entire ordeal.

By the end of the month, almost all of the people still imprisoned were released since most of the evidence against them was spectral. It is unclear whether Tituba was released in January or later in the year, but at some point, she was sold to a new master and left Salem for good.

The Supreme Court of Judicature tried several more people in early 1693 without admitting spectral evidence. The first five, who had been indicted before the first court dissolved, were all found not guilty (including Margaret Jacobs). Sixteen more people in Salem were indicted and tried, and only three of those people were found guilty. They were all pardoned by Governor Phipps. Even though the court convened a couple more times outside of Salem, by April, the nightmare of the Salem Witch Trials was all but over. In May, Phipps pardoned all of the others remaining in jail.

Even though the trials had come to an end, Salem still had to grapple with the aftermath. This was most dramatic for those who survived the accusations and their families, as well as the families of those who were executed. Even though the trials were over, Puritans still believed in witches and the Devil, and it was a mark of shame to have even been suspected of being in legion with them. Many worked for years to clear their names or the names of loved ones.

Four years later, a day of fasting and remembrance was held in Salem on January 14, 1697. Prompted by the gravity of the day, Samuel Sewall, one of the men appointed to the Court of Oyer and Terminer, apologized for his role in the trials and admitted wrongdoing in the proceedings. He was the only one of the judges who apologized, along with a few of the jurors. Later that year, the town of Salem dismissed Samuel Parris, the minister who had been in the middle of the trials. His removal was another sign that Salem wanted to distance itself from this stain on its history.

Finally, a decade after the Salem Witch Trials began, the General Court declared that all of the trials had been unlawful, but they stopped short of issuing pardons for the guilty. That came in 1711 when the colony passed a bill that also awarded financial restitution to the descendants of most of those executed for witchcraft. In the interim, more people who had been involved in the trials came forward to apologize or admit wrongdoing.

Most notably, Ann Putnam, Jr., one of the ringleaders of the young women who made the accusations in the first place, issued a public apology for her role. Her words convey some remorse about her actions and the deaths of so many people. She did not offer a direct explanation for the accusations, though. Instead, she claimed that she had been tricked by the Devil into making the accusations, and she seems to claim that at the time, she genuinely believed these lies and was convinced that her neighbors were using witchcraft on her.

One of the original causes of the Salem Witch Trials was the stark division that was growing between the town and village of Salem. The village, which was more rural and agricultural, was renamed Danvers in 1752, further distancing itself from the events of the late seventeenth century. Many of the victims had been from Salem Village, now Danvers.

No one knows where the bodies of the executed "witches" were laid to rest. Some evidence in the historical records suggest that some families claimed the bodies of their relatives after their executions and buried them quietly, while others suggest that they were thrown off of Proctor's Ledge, which was likely the site of the executions themselves. Since they were believed to be witches and had been convicted of such crimes, they were not allowed to be buried in Christian cemeteries.

As for the afflicted girls who made the accusations in the first place, most disappeared from the historical record after the trials ended. A few of them appear in later documents for various sexual deviances (adultery, having a child out of wedlock, etc.), but for the most part, it appears they went on to lead normal lives. We will likely never know if or how the events of 1692-93 may have had an ongoing impact on them.

The victims of the Salem Witch Trials have since been memorialized in and around the region where the events unfolded. One of the first was placed on the Rebecca Nurse Homestead, where Nurse lived at the time of the trials. Her descendants erected monuments in 1882 and 1895, memorializing both her and her neighbors and friends who tried to defend her against her accusers. Remains believed to be those of George Jacobs, another victim of the trials, have also been reinterred on the property.

In 1957, the state of Massachusetts formally apologized for the Salem Witch Trials and cleared the names of the remaining alleged witches who had not previously been pardoned. Then, in 1992, for the 300th anniversary, several events were held to commemorate what happened. By this point, they had become a serious part of American lore. The city of Salem dedicated a park in which they erected memorials to the victims of the Witch Trials. In Danvers (formerly the village of Salem), a memorial was also erected to the victims.

Finally, a project conducted by scholars at the University of Virginia announced in 2016 that they had determined the site of the executions was Proctor's Ledge by studying several old maps, reading first-hand accounts, and radar. A memorial now stands there as well.

For more than two hundred years, most of the residents of Salem tried to forget, ignore, or even hide the details of the Salem Witch Trials. Whether or not one believed in the Devil or witches, it was a shameful and disturbing period in their history. The Salem Witch Trials refused to be forgotten, however, and have made appearances in works of literature, film, television, and more. In the next chapter, we will examine how the Salem Witch Trials have lived on as an important piece of American history.

Chapter Nine

The Salem Witch Trials in Popular Culture

"I want the light of God, I want the sweet love of Jesus! I danced for the Devil; I saw him, I wrote in his book; I go back to Jesus; I kiss His hand. I saw Sarah Good with the Devil!"

—Excerpt from *The Crucible*, by Arthur Miller

In the grand scheme of the history of colonial New England, the Salem Witch Trials are really not important enough to have gained the notoriety that they enjoy. That said, they can be used as a very effective tool for teaching and understanding the changes happening at the time in New England as a whole.

The degree of fascination with Salem and its witches cannot be easily explained. No doubt, it combines several elements that are fascinating, including the supernatural, violence, the human mind and psyche, and history. What's more, Americans as a whole tend to be particularly interested in the Puritans, who played such a large role in the founding of their nation. That is one of the reasons that the story has been re-told so many times.

There are dozens of books written on the events in Salem. John Greenleaf Whittier wrote poems about it, and Henry Wadsworth Longfellow wrote a play about the events. One of the most famous works about the Salem Witch Trials is the play *The Crucible* by Arthur Miller, originally published in 1953. It is a fictionalized version of the events in Salem that is also widely understood to be an allegory of McCarthyism and the anti-communist movement of the era in which it was published. Miller used the Salem Witch Trials, long considered an aberration of antiquated superstitious paranoia, to make a lasting statement about events in his own times.

The Salem Witch trials have also made appearances in film and television. The first full-length film was released in 1937, and in 1996, Arthur Miller wrote a screenplay adaptation of his play for the silver screen. There are many episodes of famous television shows that feature the Salem Witch Trials, including *The Simpsons*, *Criminal Minds*, and *Saturday Night Live*. Entire seasons or parts of seasons of shows including *American Horror Story*, *Bewitched*, and *Buffy the Vampire Slayer* also feature or dramatize the Salem Witch Trials.

The city of Salem itself grapples with the memory of the trials, even to this day. On the one hand, it is a fantastic tourism draw. They have a museum dedicated to it and mark sites all around the town where the various events of 1692-1693 took place. The city also holds several special events throughout the month of October especially, leading up to Halloween. But for many, the Salem Witch Trials are a reminder of some of the worst aspects of human nature. They have also attracted some rather unsavory visitors, whose obsession with the witches of Salem has gotten out of hand.

What is certain is that Salem will never be able to shed its association with the events of 1692-93. For better or worse, it remains an important part of colonial history, American legends and lore, and universal human nature.

The Puritan migrants of New England have left an enormously influential impression on the United States. It may be fitting that the Salem

Witch Trials loom so large in their own history. After all, it encapsulates the insular, austere, and repressive society that they created.

Bibliography

Hall, David D. (2019). *The Puritans: A Transatlantic History.*

Norton, M.B. (2003). *In the Devil's Snare: The Salem Witchcraft Crisis of 1692.*

Roach, M.K. (2004). *The Salem Witch Trials: A Day-by-Day Chronicle of a Community Under Siege.*

Roach, M.K. (2013). *Six Women of Salem: The Untold Story of the Accused and Their Accusers in the Salem Witch Trials.*

Salem Witch Museum Online. (2021). Accessed at https://www.salemwitchmuseum.com.

Schiff, Stacy. (2015). *The Witches: Salem, 1692.*

Taylor, A. (2002). *American Colonies: The Settling of North America.*

University of Virginia. (2018). "The Salem Witch Trials Documentary Archive and Transcription

Project." Accessed
http://salem.lib.virginia.edu/home.html.